# A Pocket [...]
# to Wa[...]

by

# CHARLES SMITH

**Mowbray**
LONDON & OXFORD

Copyright © Charles Smith 1988

ISBN 0 264 67135 X

First published 1988
by A.R. Mowbray & Co. Ltd
Saint Thomas House, Becket Street,
Oxford, OX1 1SJ

All rights reserved. No part of this publication
may be reproduced, stored in a retrieval system,
or transmitted, in any form or by any means,
electronic, mechanical, photocopying, recording,
or otherwise, without the prior permission in writing
from the publisher, A.R. Mowbray & Co. Ltd.

Typeset by Comersgate Art Studios, Oxford

Printed in Great Britain by Redwood Burn Ltd,
Trowbridge

**British Library Cataloguing in Publication Data**

Smith, Charles
 A pocket guide to Walsingham. —— (Mowbrays
 pocket guides).
 1. Norfolk. Walsingham. Visitors' guides
 I. Title
 914.26'12
 ISBN 0–264–67135–X

ISBN 0-264-67

# CONTENTS

| | |
|---|---:|
| *Introduction* | page 1 |
| *A Little History* | 3 |
| *The Anglican Shrine* | 13 |
| *Development of Roman Catholic Pilgrimages* | 16 |
| *Walsingham and Ecumenism* | 19 |
| *Orthodox, Methodists and others* | 21 |
| *Why?* | 24 |
| *Mary in the Church* | 29 |
| *A Tour of the Village* | 31 |
| *Further Afield* | 45 |
| *To be a Pilgrim* | 47 |
| *Getting to Walsingham* | 50 |
| *Some Prayers and Devotions* | 54 |

# ACKNOWLEDGMENTS

A pocket guide might seem a very simple compilation, but the complexities of Walsingham call for many enquiries and contacts. I am very grateful to the Administrator and Bursar of the Anglican Shrine, and to the Director of the Roman Catholic Shrine and his staff for the time they have given me and for many helpful comments. Especially I am grateful for access to some unpublished correspondence about the early days of the Roman Catholic revival. Fr David of the Orthodox church gave me much help, and the pastor of the Walsingham Methodist church information which otherwise I would have found quite inaccessible.

The pictures come from the records of the two shrines, from Mr Kenneth Faircloth, photographer, of Walsingham, and from Mr Alex Niedzwecki. The sketch of the Methodist church is by Mrs Janet Beckett, of Wells next the Sea, who kindly gave me permission to print it.

Many friends at both shrines, and others who know Walsingham, have checked the manuscript for factual errors. Any which remain are my own fault, but in a place where pious fiction can so easily be allowed to replace fact, one is sometimes unconscious of what one has imbibed.

**Charles Smith**

# INTRODUCTION

Norfolk is not the most easily accessible holiday area, and some believe it is cold and bleak. Yet it is greatly loved by those who have come to appreciate its charms, the wide skies, the open spaces, the marshes and the fresh north sea breezes. There are, too, the tiny villages, with their brick and flint houses and Dutch gables, the great churches dominating the landscape and the ruins of other churches, sometimes a reminder of villages which disappeared with the black death in the fourteenth century. Cley-next-the-Sea, Cawston, Reepham, Swaffham, Salle, Blakeney all have their fascination, but the great church of Walsingham, or rather, the churches of Walsingham, are second to none. The village holds many surprises for the visitor who knows nothing of its history, nor of the thousands who flock there today, as they have done throughout most of its history. At the beginning of this century, travel books on East Anglia told of its past glories, sometimes with a certain nostalgia for a more romantic age, and regretted its passing, never suspecting that within a few years the glory would return, and English people would again come to 'England's Nazareth' (as it was once called) in large numbers.

You may visit Walsingham because of its history, and there are historic churches, buildings and ruins enough to make it worth while on that score alone. You may go there because it is a beautiful village in unspoilt country, and no tour of North Norfolk is complete without it. But that does not explain its attraction. It is a living religious centre, of great attractiveness and increasing importance in a century always regarded as irreligious, and a significant place of pilgrimage.

A pilgrimage is something more than a tourist excursion. It is a journey with a serious purpose, and satisfies a deep human desire to gaze on the sights the great and holy once saw, and to walk in their footsteps. Another kind of pilgrimage may take us to the Normandy or Anzio beaches, or perhaps to our birthplace, or the house where some notable man or woman we admire once lived. The instinct behind it is deeper than mere curiosity, and there is always an element of veneration and of resolution. In their journey Christians see an acted parable of their way through this world to God — their earthly pilgrimage. From earliest days Christians went on pilgrimage to the Holy Land, in spite of the difficulties and dangers, and they went to the tombs of the martyrs and saints. In England in days gone by, the Shrine of St Thomas Becket in Canterbury Cathedral was famous, and no doubt owing to Chaucer's *Canterbury Tales* comes most readily to mind, but the Walsingham pilgrimage was even more popular. If you come to Walsingham as a pilgrim you will understand something of the thoughts of our ancestors who travelled the 'Walsingham way'. If you come as a tourist or sightseer, not feeling that you can claim the name of 'pilgrim', it is worth while trying to enter into the thoughts and motives of those who made the shrine what it was, and is. Not everyone who comes to Walsingham would claim to be a person of great faith, or even to be a practising Christian, but many have found something which speaks to them, contrary to all their expectations. Perhaps we gain something from following in so long a tradition of faith.

# A Little History

The story of Walsingham begins before the Norman Conquest. Although the date has been questioned, the generally accepted date for the beginning of the shrine was during the reign of Edward the Confessor, in the year 1061. It is said that the lady of the manor of Walsingham, Richeldis de Faverches, saw a vision of the Blessed Virgin Mary and was shown a replica of the holy house of Nazareth in which Mary received the visit of the Archangel Gabriel according to St Luke's gospel (chapter 2, vv. 26-38), to which the child Jesus was brought, and in which he grew up. The story is told in the *Ballad of Walsingham*, a fifteenth century manuscript in the library of Magdalene College, Cambridge. In a sceptical age no doubt, reactions to the story will vary, but the eleventh century was not a sceptical age, and even in our own days claims to such experiences have been made in France, Portugal, Yugoslavia, Egypt and elsewhere. It is very difficult to gainsay or disprove them, although both ecclesiastical and secular authorities can find them embarrassing. The supernatural *does* impinge on our material, physical life, and we would do well to accept this as a fact. We do not have to put our critical faculties to sleep, but there are many things beyond our explanation, and many would claim that this is certainly true at Walsingham. Not least remarkable is the revival in this century of a devotion and a place of pilgrimage which had seemed completely dead. There is nothing inherently improbable in the story of Richeldis de Faverches, explain it as we will. It was a time when men's minds were turning towards the Holy Land, and the holy places, Nazareth among them, then in the hands of the Moslems. When the First Crusade was preached in 1095, thousands went to the Holy Land. The Holy House of Loreto which has a similar devotion, was, apparently, founded at the end of the thirteenth century. It has been suggested that Walsingham was a pale imitation of Loreto, but the dates contradict that allegation. Rather, they are parallel developments, showing what was in the minds of European men and women at that time.

It is worth noting that the centre of Walsingham has always been the Holy House. In the beginning there may have been no statue inside it, although the lack was, no doubt, soon repaired. It may be that a rough wooden statue was placed inside the little house, and became the prototype of those the visitor will recognise all over the village, and in many churches throughout the world as 'Our Lady of Walsingham'. She is depicted on the walls of the great church at Nazareth, and there is a statue in the cathedral of Santiago de Compostela. Perhaps it all goes back to that Saxon lady, nearly a thousand years ago. Richeldis built her little house of wood, and in spite of the almost irresistible urge to rebuild, to pull down inferior structures and to put up something 'more worthy', the little wooden house remained all through the middle ages. After a time it was covered with a stone structure to protect it, but it was to the 'Holy House' that pilgrims flocked.

Associated with the shrine was a spring of water, in which pilgrims would bathe. Archaeologists say that the wells (there are two) were pre-Christian, and only at a later stage associated with the shrine. The legend tells that Richeldis planned to build her little house close to the wells, but it was miraculously moved to a different spot. There has been considerable argument about the whereabouts of the well or wells. When the present Anglican shrine was bulit in the 1930's, foundations of ancient buildings were found, and a well, considered to be of Saxon masonry and filled with rubble which included a number of shoes from the Tudor period. Those responsible jumped to the conclusion that they had discovered the original holy well and the original site of the Holy House of Walsingham. Later excavations, however, have shown, fairly conclusively, that although the shrine was on the north side of the priory church, it was not so far distant, and the well was inside the walls of Walsingham Abbey, though, it is true, not very far from the modern shrine.

Geoffrey de Faeverches, the son of Richeldis, about to go to the Holy Land on pilgrimage or crusade, arranged for the 'institution of a religious order' at the chapel his mother had founded. As a result, the Augustinians came to Walsingham, and their priory church, whose remains may still be seen, was founded. There have been two churches on the site. The first, a Norman church, started, probably, during the second half of the twelfth century, and then a complete rebuilding of the whole priory carried out during the thirteenth century. The most dramatic remain is the east window of the priory church, but we will find others.

If we are to understand the various buildings in Walsingham, we must remember that the Holy House which Richeldis had built was never included within the church, but remained a separate building on its north side. It was covered and protected with a stone structure — the 'new work' to which contemporaries refer — in the middle of the fifteenth century. Other buildings remain which were clearly part of the priory. If it is agreed that it was a mistake to regard the present Anglican shrine as being on the site of the original Holy House, the foundations left exposed there, may have been associated with it in some other way.

In 1346 the Franciscans came to Walsingham and founded the Friary, remains of which may still be seen. Their presence, although not very welcome to the Augustinians who had long been installed, and the number of inns reported in the village, indicate the popularity of Walsingham. Numbers had increased steadily since the Norman Conquest. At first, no doubt, pilgrims came from nearby, but soon they were coming from all over England and the continent. Medieval men and women were happy to find another shrine to which they could go on pilgrimage. Henry III, the first royal pilgrim, came in 1226, and his successors followed. Edward I had a great devotion to the shrine and came at least twelve times.

'And kings, lord and commons, their homage would
    pay
And the burning of tapers turned night into day',
as a popular modern pilgrimage hymn says. Men came along certain clear routes, and pilgrim chapels and rest houses were built for their benefit along the way. Only two chapels remain — the Chapel of the Red Mount in King's Lynn, and the Slipper Chapel in Houghton St Giles, very close to Walsingham, which houses the modern Roman Catholic shrine.

## Destruction of the shrine

It seemed that this popularity and royal favour were set to continue under the Tudor monarchs, for Henry VII had a great devotion to Our Lady of Walsingham. After the defeat of Lambert Simnel he sent his standard to the shrine 'as a memorial of the favour he had received from God'. His son, Henry VIII, inherited this devotion and came to the shrine in 1511, the last English king to do so. He is reported to have stayed on this occasion at East Barsham manor. He paid money to help maintain the shrine: a candle was kept burning for him, for which he paid 43s.4d. annually, and a chaplain said mass for him, for which he paid £10. His wife, Catherine of Aragon, shared his devotion. A letter to Henry, after his victory over the Scots in 1513, says '. . . with this I make an end . . . and now go to Our Lady of Walsingham that I promised so long ago to see'. She held the manors of Great and Little Walsingham, and in her will, dated 1536, provided '. . . that some personage go to Our Lady of Walsingham in pilgrimage, and in going, by the way to deal twenty nobles'. This charitable provision of Queen Catherine demonstrates that the religious and spiritual purpose of pilgrimage was not entirely forgotten, and it is possible to exaggerate the corruption at the end of the Middle Ages. But corruption there undoubtedly was, in Walsingham no less than elsewhere.

Henry VIII's suppression of the monasteries is a familiar part of English history. The smaller monasteries were closed first, and the larger ones followed. The Priory of Walsingham was one of the former, and had the added attraction of being exceedingly rich through the offerings of pilgrims. The King's commissioners directed their attention to it in 1538, and the Prior, Richard Vowell, surrendered everything without demur. He received a good pension for his co-operation, as did the other members of the community. The sub-prior, however, Roger Mileham, was among a small group of villagers who showed some signs of resisting. He and one other were executed in a field still called the Martyrs' Field behind the railway station. He is commemorated by the name of one of the old houses in the Common Place. The celebrated image of the Blessed Virgin was taken to London and burnt at Chelsea, while the Holy House was destroyed and the site of the priory given to one Thomas Sydney and his wife. As with other monastic buildings, it soon fell into ruins and the stone was used by the owners of the property and others to build their own houses. Many a stone from the old priory still makes up Walsingham houses! The big house became known as 'Walsingham Abbey' but this has no connection with the medieval foundation which was always a Priory. The verses, often attributed to St Philip Howard,* at about this time have become part of the Walsingham story, and give some sense of the desolation of those years

> Bitter, bitter oh to behoulde
> The grass to growe
> Where the walls of Walsingham
> So stately did show.

A period of almost total eclipse began. The visitor will find many remains of the village's great past, a fine doorway or window here, a moulding there, but three to four hundred years from the Reformation to the early

---

* Attractive as this attribution is, there seems very good ground for questioning it. It seems to be based on the fact that it is bound up with some material by St Philip in a volume in the Bodleian Library, Oxford.

twentieth century in which it was completely neglected without any respect for its history have, unhappily, destroyed a good deal.

There was almost complete silence during this period. No doubt the occasional pilgrim came in a spirit of faith, but for most men and women, the 'Age of Reason' had succeeded the religious wars of the sixteenth and seventeenth centuries. Pilgrimage and the lively faith from which it sprang seemed to have died out long ago. Perhaps the most significant event of the eighteenth century was the visit of John Wesley, who preached in Walsingham at two in the afternoon of Tuesday, 30 October, 1781. His comment in his *Journal* is worth recording. 'Afterwards I walked over what is left of the famous Abbey, the east end of which is still standing. We then went to the Friary; the cloisters and chapel whereof are almost entire. Had there been a grain of virtue or public spirit in Henry the Eighth, these noble buildings need not have run to ruin.'

## Revival

The Romantic movement of the early nineteenth century was a literary and not a religious movement, but since it concerned itself with things medieval, inevitably roused an interest in ecclesiastical matters, however little they may have been understood. This had an effect on the revival of Catholicism which occurred during the century. The Catholic Emancipation Act of 1829 removed most of the legal disabilities under which Roman Catholics had suffered for three centuries, and introduced a period of renewed activity. In the established church, the Oxford Movement, usually reckoned as beginning in

1833, was primarily an academic and theological movement, but soon affected the practice of religion in parishes all over the country. It sought to bring back much that its supporters believed had been unjustifiably suppressed in the sixteenth century. In both churches, there was a great interest in pre-Reformation England, and a desire to restore medieval religious life wherever possible. Such was the background to the renewal of interest in the Shrine of Our Lady of Walsingham.

Walsingham Abbey had for some years been in the hands of the Lee-Warner family, some of whose members were influenced by the Oxford Movement. One of these, James Lee-Warner, became Vicar of Walsingham, and undertook excavations on the site of the Priory church in the early 1850's. It may have been reports of these excavations which caused the Reverend Arthur Douglas Wagner, a great church builder in the Brighton area, to incorporate in his new church at Buxted, Sussex, a Lady Chapel according to the recorded measurements of the Holy House at Walsingham. Alfred Hope Patten, the future Vicar of Walsingham, lived in Brighton, often visited Buxted, and must have seen what was popularly known as 'the Walsingham chapel'. The seeds of future developments may have been sown there.

Revival of another kind was taking place in Norfolk. The Roman Catholic parish priest of King's Lynn, the Reverend George Wrigglesworth, had to build a new church to replace one which was fast falling into ruins. It is said that he received contributions from His Royal Highness Edward, Prince of Wales (the future Edward VII), who was ashamed of the poor condition of the church to which he often accompanied his Roman Catholic guests from Sandringham House. Fr Wrigglesworth incorporated in his church a Lady Chapel in honour of the Holy House at Nazareth, built according to the measurements of the Holy House of Loreto, in Northern Italy. This was to be the centre of revived devotion to Our Lady of Walsingham, to which Pope Leo XIII had given his approval. A statue to be placed in the chapel was carved at Oberammergau, and at the Pope's suggestion was based on a picture in the church of St Maria in Cosmedin in Rome. It was regarded as suitable, since this had been the titular church of Cardinal Reginald Pole, the last Archbishop of Canterbury to be in communion with Rome. This, the first post-Reformation shrine of Our Lady of Walsingham, may still be visited.

Meanwhile, a remarkable lady, with that kind of devout eccentricity often to be found among wealthy Victorians, had turned her attention to Walsingham. Miss Charlotte Boyd was an ardent enthusiast for the cause of the Oxford Movement, especially for the revival of the Benedictine life. She came to Walsingham in the hope of securing Walsingham Abbey as a home for some nuns. The project failed, but she did buy the Chapel of St Catherine (the 'Slipper Chapel'), at that time used as a farm building. She restored it — beautifully — and, having become a Roman Catholic in Bruges in 1895, gave it into the custody of the Benedictines of Downside.

This event, and the completion of the new church in King's Lynn, occurred in 1896-7, and the devotion to Our Lady of Walsingham was inaugurated on 19 August 1897, with great festivity. The statue arrived at the railway station, and was carried in procession to its place in the church. The following day, 20 August, a pilgrimage 'with contingents from Lynn, Norwich, Beccles and other places' went to the restored Slipper Chapel. This, the first public pilgrimage since the sixteenth century, was organised by the recently founded Guild of Our Lady of

Ransom, which has ever since been active in the encouragement of pilgrimages to Walsingham. The actual shrine continued to be in the church in King's Lynn, already officially designated as the Shrine of Our Lady of Walsingham. There is no record of any public pilgrimage to Walsingham itself after 1897, but groups of pilgrims made their way to the Slipper Chapel where a caretaker admitted them and to the village.

In 1903 Charlotte Boyd offered the Slipper Chapel and priest's house to the Bishop of Northampton for the £2,000 it had cost her, but Bishop Riddell could not avail himself of the offer. Again, Launcelot Lee-Warner, who had become a Roman Catholic, wrote to the bishop, promising that if he were to inherit the family property at Walsingham, as was quite possible, he would return it to the Church. This however was not to be, and the difficulty of the Shrine already established at King's Lynn continued until 1934. Meanwhile, remarkable events had occurred in the village.

# The Anglican Shrine

In 1921, a very remarkable new Vicar, Alfred Hope Patten, came to Walsingham. He was an ardent and effective parish priest and set about restoring Walsingham and its shrine to their ancient splendour. A statue was carved and placed in the Guilds' Chapel on the north side of the parish church, and it is the proud boast of the Anglican shrine that nightly rosary and intercessions have never been interrupted since that day. The first trickle of pilgrims started coming once more in 1922.

It was clear, for various reasons, that the statue and shrine could not remain in the parish church — they had never been there in any case, even in the 'old days'. Consequently some ground was bought, and given by Sir William Milner, a Yorkshire baronet, and the work of rebuilding the Shrine and Holy House of Our Lady of Walsingham was begun. The measurements of the original shrine, recorded by William of Worcester at the end of the fifteenth century, were closely followed, but the building was of brick and plaster, not of wood. The whole was enclosed in an outer building, like the medieval shrine at the time of its destruction. During this building, the well, still enclosed within the walls of the shrine, and the foundations, left exposed underneath it, were discovered. This gave rise to considerable excitement, and many people at the time concluded that this was the site of the original shrine, a view which has since been abandoned as a result of further excavation. The building was consecrated on 15 October 1931, and seven years later, in June 1938, the church was further extended. The model followed was as close as possible to that depicted on the medieval seal, with a central lantern. Inside, there are fifteen altars, each in honour of one of the great events ('mysteries') in the life of our Lord and his Mother. Stones from many holy places, cathedrals and shrines all over the world were incorporated, and may be seen with the name of their place of origin carved on them. The stone carving on piscinas, holy water stoups etc. was carried out by local people under the inspiration of Hope Patten, who had a particular ability to inspire other people with his own enthusiasm. The wall paintings were for the most part executed by Enid Chadwick, an artist who devoted her skill to the service of the Shrine.

Hope Patten died suddenly in 1958, and his body was laid in the churchyard of the parish church. A little later the cloister on the north side, with the effigy of the 'Restorer of the Shrine', was built as a memorial. This began to let in more light, and the work was completed in 1972, when the Jubilee Cloister on the south side was added to commemorate the first fifty years since the restoration of the devotion in Walsingham.

Further old cottages on the south side of the new building were bought and converted into the College of St Augustine, to house the clergy who serve the shrine and others. Cottages on the north side, became the Hospice of Our Lady, Star of the Sea, to house pilgrims. These have needed further expansion with the passage of years, and since the supply of old cottages is not unlimited, new buildings have been added. Care has been taken to preserve the medieval feel of the original hospice. More recently St Joseph's Wing has been added to provide for the sick and disabled, opened by the Duchess of Kent in October 1985. The existing accommodation built only some fifteen years previously, was already inadequate to the demand. Close by is the Priory of Our Lady, with its own chapel, the home of the Sisters who work for the shrine. All these stand in beautifully kept grounds.

The shrine is cared for by a priest administrator and his assistant(s). Responsibility for it rests upon the College of Guardians, some clerical and some laymen, whose names may be found painted on the stalls of the shrine church. Although, of course, its clergy are authorised and licenced by the Bishop of Norwich, the shrine remains private property, as with other private chapels. Like many important movements in English religion, it started as a private effort through the devotion and sacrifice of individuals and has come to be accepted by all.

# Development of Roman Catholic Pilgrimages

The development of the Roman Catholic Shrine has been quite different. It has been, at least in modern times, an official project. That probably tells us a good deal about the way in which the two churches work.

After the gift of the Slipper Chapel in 1897, nothing public or official happened until 1934. In that year it was agreed that the devotion should be transferred from the chapel in King's Lynn and Cardinal Bourne, Archbishop of Westminster, led a pilgrimage of some 10,000 people to Walsingham — the biggest yet — and the Slipper Chapel became in truth the National Shrine of Our Lady. To begin with, the fact that it was a mile outside the village seemed a disadvantage, but that has been turned to advantage, and the walk along the 'holy mile' by the banks of the Stiffkey, has become an integral part of the pilgrimage to most Roman Catholics. In 1938, the Slipper Chapel was consecrated once more, and an enormous children's pilgrimage was some token of things to come. In those days, when the Slipper Chapel stood alone in the Norfolk fields, it had a charm of its own, which the careful restoration of the interior maintained. In the same year the sacristy and a small chapel of the Holy Ghost was added. Then came the war when Walsingham, being in a highly protected coastal zone, was closed to visitors. Nevertheless, members of the American forces, and later, prisoners of war, were able to keep the devotion alive and, on 17 May 1945, only a few days after the end of the war in Europe, members of the American forces were able to assist at a Mass celebrated on the site of the old high altar of Walsingham Priory church.

After the experience of the second great war there was a fresh realisation among European Christians of the urgency of praying and working for peace. Consequently, a great international pilgrimage for peace was organised to Vézelay, in Burgundy. The following year, 1948, a British pilgrimage to Walsingham was organised, and the fourteen large crosses now set up as the Stations of the Cross in the grounds surrounding the Slipper Chapel were carried by groups from all over the country. In direct succession to this pilgrimage, a similar cross-bearing pilgrimage organised by students and known as Student Cross is organised each Holy Week. It is completely ecumenical, and bearing four crosses starts from four agreed points, arriving in Walsingham on Good Friday. The presence of the parties of students adds a great deal to the gaiety of the celebration of the resurrection in Walsingham year by year.

The years following World War II saw a great emphasis on devotion to Mary and on Mariology, the theological consideration of her place in the scheme of redemption. This reached its climax in the definition of the doctrine of the Assumption by Pope Pius XII in 1950, and the Marian Year in 1954, marking the centenary of the definition of the Immaculate Conception. In such times, the shrine at Walsingham came into its own, and on 15 August, 1954, the statue of Our Lady of Walsingham was crowned by the Apostolic Delegate, Archbishop O'Hara, on behalf of the Pope. It seemed that reparation had been made for the deliberate desecration under Henry VIII.

During these years, numbers of pilgrims were continually increasing, and it was essential to provide facilities for them. Consequently, the pilgrim centre was opened on land surrounding the Slipper Chapel. It was much criticised as being out of keeping with the countryside and with the chapel and older buildings, but the needs of modern pilgrims must be met, and more recently the centre has been adapted to its surroundings. All but the tiniest groups had to be catered for in the open air, and there had been various temporary arrangements. In 1982, however, the Chapel of Reconciliation was built, and is a valuable addition to the buildings on the site. Its title is an indication of the kind of work associated with Walsingham in recent years, and the chapel has already held many notable gatherings.

Successive bishops of Northampton did a great deal to ensure the development of the Shrine, but it now comes within the boundaries of the diocese of East Anglia, created in 1976. Since 1968, the shrine has been cared for by the Marist Fathers.

# Walsingham and Ecumenism

Perhaps the high water mark of modern devotion to Our Lady of Walsingham came on 29 May 1982, when the statue from the Slipper Chapel was taken to the Wembley Stadium to be venerated by Pope John Paul II on his visit to Britain. It was carried into the arena by the Director of the Roman Catholic Shrine and the Administrator of the Anglican Shrine accompanied by people from the village, and was received with great acclamation. It remained on the altar throughout the Papal Mass.

Signposts to Walsingham often confuse, and many a coachload of pilgrims has arrived at the 'wrong' shrine. Isn't it a pity there are TWO shrines in Walsingham? It *does* confuse some people, of course, and in the past, we must admit, there has been a good deal of misunderstanding and misrepresentation. It only reflects the state of religion in England! Now, happily, there is complete cooperation between the two shrines. As Bishop Clark of East Anglia once said, there is really only one shrine in Walsingham, it is Walsingham itself; there are several centres of devotion. Let us repeat: the shrine in the village is administered by Anglicans, i.e. members of the Church of England, the Slipper Chapel and all its buildings belong to the Roman Catholic authorities.

Members of each church are encouraged to visit the centre of devotion of the other and to pray for the unity of Christians. On any great occasion, Anglican or Roman Catholic, you will see representatives of the other body in the processions etc. Now that the site of the original shrine has been more or less universally agreed, it may be that, at some remote future date, if reunion has not come by that time, a joint shrine will be built on the original spot, and the two present centres seen as steps on the way.

# Orthodox, Methodists and Others

It is not only in relations between Anglicans and Roman Catholics that Walsingham has great opportunities. There is also an Orthodox Church of St Seraphim, under the jurisdiction of the Russian Patriarchate, and cared for by a brotherhood of the Orthodox Church. There is also an Orthodox chapel in the Anglican Shrine and Orthodox pilgrims are frequent visitors. Newcomers to Walsingham are often surprised to hear unfamiliar strains of Orthodox liturgies and hymns in the Shrine, and to meet bearded Orthodox priests in the streets of the village. Contrary to widespread belief, devotion to the Mother of Jesus is found to be a uniting rather than a divisive factor in ecumenical relations. That this should be true of certain churches may not be surprising, but the English Free Churches might be expected to stand apart from such institutions as the shrines at Walsingham. That is no longer so, for Christian people of all denominations realise that here is a holy place, and they are happy to come to pray. Pilgrims are encouraged to visit the historic Methodist church, and once a year a procession goes round the village visiting all the holy places — Anglican, Methodist, Roman Catholic and Orthodox. Members of each communion play their part, in their own way, in the spiritual and religious life of England's Nazareth. The Anglican shrine is used for conferences and prayer by several free church groups.

To live in the village of Walsingham is to understand how prayer and a faith in the Incarnation, which all

The Methodist Church, Little Walsingham

Christians share, enable men and women of different traditions to overcome the barriers which seemed to divide them. Walsingham is above all else a shrine of the Incarnation; that unites all Christians. Its veneration for the Mother of Jesus follows from that, and in this village it is difficult to believe that she should ever have seemed a cause of dissension. There are, of course, some, perhaps many, whose prejudice against any devotion to the Blessed Virgin is so strong that they cannot see how others can share in it, but increasingly, as the central convictions of the Christian faith are allowed to stand out, Mary is seen as the Mother of Him who was God. This can only unite Christians.

# Why?

What is the attraction of Walsingham? It is an attractive village, but there are many other such villages in Norfolk. It has an interesting history, associated with great names and great events, and as a result, it has some impressive buildings, as well as a large number of typical Norfolk houses. But that is not why people come here in such large numbers, and come again and again.

## A place of prayer

Only a small proportion (one of the lowest in Europe) of the people of England go to church regularly, a large number of them still pray or try to pray, or would like to pray. But prayer is not easy. The poet T.S. Eliot wrote of another holy place as one '. . . where prayer has been valid'. That is true of Walsingham, and people come in their thousands just to pray. There are other such places in the world. We need not be ashamed to admit that we cannot pray everywhere. We need to use all the helps we can, and when we have become men and women of prayer we may be able to pray anywhere. If God seems more real to us in some places than in others, let us be thankful for it. Apparently it has always been like that: the Bible is full of accounts of such places. In the Old Testament, Jacob said 'Truly the Lord is in this place, and I never knew it! This is nothing less than a house of God; this is the gate of heaven' (Genesis 28.16-17 J.B.). If we apply this insight to our own pilgrimage we will try not merely to look at the shrines, but try to pray in them, using our own words, or some of the prayers printed at the end of this book which are used by other pilgrims. Listen to T.S. Eliot again '... You are not here to verify, Instruct yourself, or inform curiosity Or carry report. You are here to kneel ... And prayer is more Than an order of words.' (Little Gidding). Perhaps your prayer will be better if you do not try to use words, but simply remain silent as thousands, probably millions, have done before you, in the Holy House or Slipper Chapel, or as you walk through the lanes and streets. It helps, of course, if you are in a party and everyone remains silent or prays together, but one source of the prayerfulness of the place is the fact that we are joining with those who have gone before us, and especially with the Mother of Jesus, 'higher than the cherubim, more glorious than the seraphim', who is honoured here, and with all the saints. That comes home to us with special force in Walsingham.

This has been a place for a particular kind of prayer, the prayer in which we ask for things. To regard that as the only kind of prayer is to misunderstand it, but it is equally wrong to refuse to ask for what we need when we pray. To recognise particular answers to prayer is a very personal and private matter, but there are many people who are confident that their prayer offered here has been answered. Your own petition will be remembered at the shrines if you ask, but you must ask with faith. Miracles DO happen, but we do not always recognise them.

## An act of faith

That brings us to another of the great attractions of Walsingham. It is a place of *faith*. The late twentieth century, especially in our part of the world, seems to have lost faith, and as a result has lost hope too. Here there is an assertion of a bold and confident faith, built upon one of the central convictions of the Christian religion, that

God became man, the Word was made flesh, and dwelt among us, and he took a young Jewish girl as his Mother, the girl called Mary. We need to have the truth of that driven home for us over and over again, and Walsingham does just that. The very materialism, the crudity even, of the statues etc. we see about the place help to remind us that material things can convey the truth about God to us — Christians must never become too 'spiritual' and treat visible, material things as if they did not matter. The Incarnation is the gospel our world needs to hear, for it teaches that human nature can be raised to great heights. Men and women are made to be united to God, and not to be trampled on or exploited, degraded or despised. There is nobody whom we must not honour, for he raises up the humble and meek as he raised Mary. Quite a number of people who had lost their faith have found it again at Walsingham. It speaks to our twentieth century in a remarkable way, when discussion and argument get us nowhere. To go to an ancient pilgrimage centre is to take part in a shared experience, and our experiences of faith may point beyond bald reason. Perhaps experiencing the love of God in a young mother with her Child, and looking at it with a great multitude of people of all centuries, not least along with a great multitude of very modern people, may do something to revive or strengthen our own faith.

## A place for healing

Like many or most of the great Christian shrines, Walsingham is also a place of healing. The most famous healing shrine in the modern church is Lourdes. There, careful record is kept of all cases in which healing of the sick and disabled seems to have occurred. Claim of a miracle is made only after the most careful investigation and where there could be no human explanation of the cure. But there are many who come away from Lourdes confident that they have been healed there, or have been helped in some other way. So it is with Walsingham. It would be a serious misunderstanding to imagine that God only operates when a notable healing occurs. One of the deepest truths we have to learn about ourselves is that body and spirit are one whole person, and healing of the spirit or soul is more important than healing of the body, important as that is. The sick come to Walsingham, or to any pilgrim centre, asking for what it may please God to give them, whether it be a help to carry their cross, some spiritual gift — greater faith, or vision, or patience — some relief of their pain, or a complete cure. Both Anglican and Roman Catholic shrines have special provision for the sick and disabled, and there are always such people in pilgrimage parties, as well as pilgrimages from time to time specially for them. The Church's important work of healing is becoming increasingly recognised as people turn away from an entirely materialistic idea of what man is: we all need that wholeness of our complete human nature of which Jesus spoke. You will know what you lack for wholeness, and do not hesitate to ask for it through prayer, the sacrament of the sick or any other means that God may use.

## Renewal

Finally, Walsingham attracts people because it speaks, and is an example of, renewal in the life of the Church. Nothing could have seemed more dead than this village in 1920. The glimmerings of new life were so faint that nobody noticed it. They seemed to spring from nostalgia for the past, a sort of religious romanticism which idealised the Middle Ages. Within the lifetime of many people, it has become a great spiritual centre, bearing witness to the reality of the things of the Spirit, and the power of faith in Jesus the Son of Mary.

Many of those who come find that here things are looked at from a different angle. What might seem artificial or unreal at home seems very real here. 'I would never have believed that I would be so impressed. I thought it was not the kind of thing to attract modern people, but I have found I was wrong.' That is a typical reaction from one reluctant pilgrim, who has learnt to love Walsingham.

Our Lady of Walsingham. The statue in the Slipper Chapel.

The Anglican Shrine.

Interior of the Slipper Chapel.

(*overleaf*) A procession sets out for the Slipper Chapel.

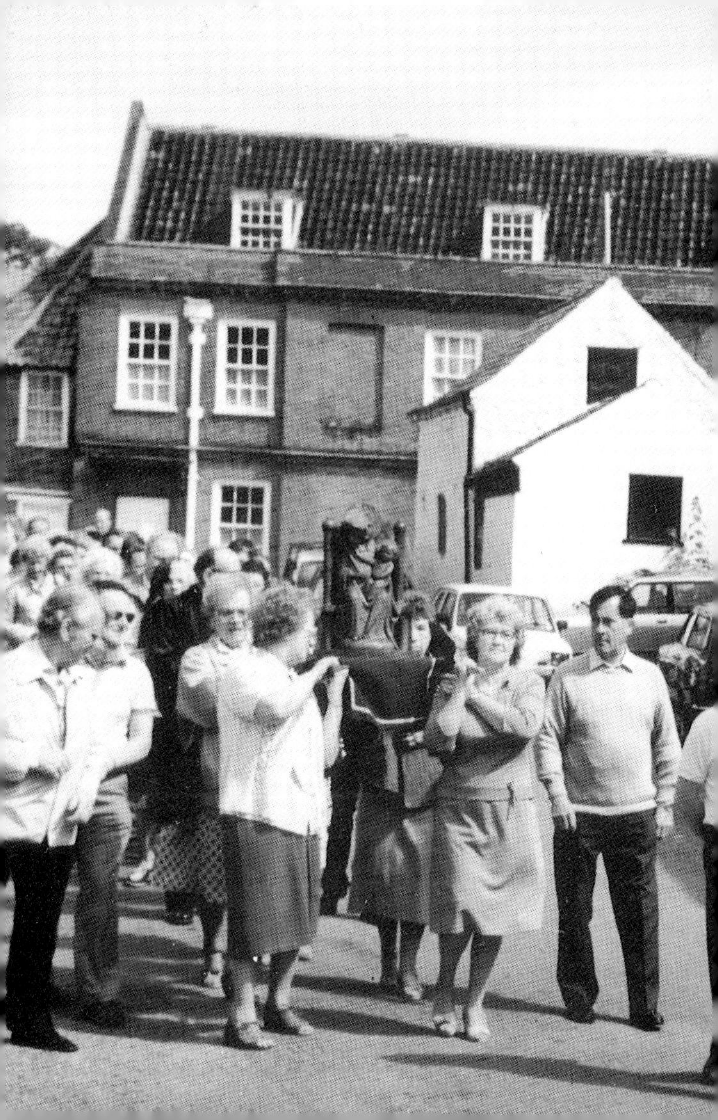

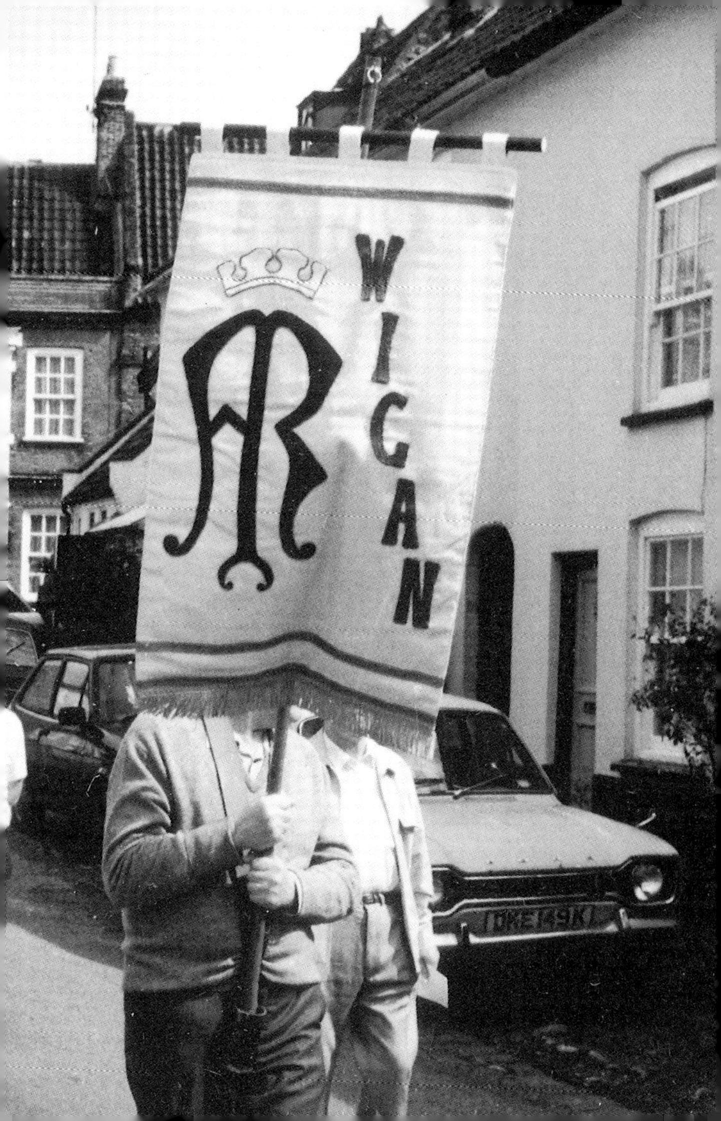
WIGAN

The ruined east window of the medieval Augustinian priory.

Exterior of the Holy House in the Anglican Shrine.

Exterior of the Slipper Chapel.

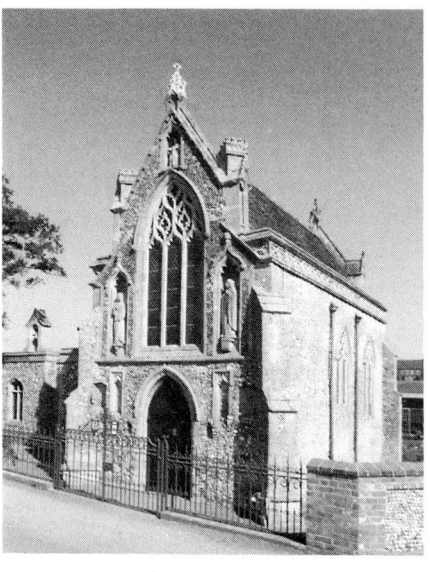

An Orthodox procession in the streets of Walsingham.

# Mary in the Church

It seems strange to Christians from other countries that the Blessed Virgin has little or no place in the religion of many English people. Whereas to the typical French, Italian or Spanish Christian, to the Russian, the Serb or the Greek, Mary is a living presence and a helper, many an English churchgoer gives little thought to her, and would never dream of asking her prayers. Even in Roman Catholic circles, there are some in post Vatican II days who have been influenced by this very English, indeed British, atmosphere. It was not always so, for in the Middle Ages England was known as 'Mary's Dowry' and there were many churches dedicated to her. In very recent times, in this as in many other matters, people are trying to get behind the prejudices and misunderstandings of the past, and find where they went wrong. Mary must have had a great influence on her son and the forming of his human mind. He learnt his prayers from her, and she was closer to him than any other human being. To honour Jesus as God, leads us to honour Mary. It was one of the great councils of the Church, in the year A.D. 431, which gave her the title of 'Theotokos', 'Mother of God'. But Mary was nothing in herself, she became what she was and is through the grace of God, the supreme example of what God, through Jesus Christ, is trying to do in every human being. Mary is one of us, but one of us who cooperates with God in the divine scheme to rescue the human race and restore all things when, at the Annunciation, she says 'Behold the handmaid of the Lord, be it done to me according to your word', Walsingham's shrine commemorates that event above everything else, and asks that we too might cooperate with God in his plan for us and for his world. Mary, too, was the beginning of the Church. She made that supremely generous and humble response to God which all Christians try to make, and she became full of the grace of God. She entered into the sufferings of her Son when she stood by the cross on Good Friday, and she was with the Apostles when they waited for the coming of the Holy Spirit.

It has been said that there is not very much about Mary in the New Testament. That simply is not true. Hers is not an active role like Peter's or Paul's, but she is there at the supreme moments, and her quiet role is just such as most Christians have to play. 'Blessed is she who believed, for those things which were told her by the Lord will be fulfilled' said Elizabeth, 'Blessed are they who hear the word of God and keep it' said Jesus, Mary is indeed 'blessed among women'.

There are Christians who do not feel they can ask Mary for her prayers or her help in the way such requests are made at Walsingham. That seems a perfectly natural thing to do for *most* Christians, for she is 'in Christ', very close to him, and it would seem strange not to ask for her prayers, just as we ask for the prayers of our friends or of people we believe to be very holy. But if you find it strange and unnatural, be content with honouring the Mother of the Lord, and she will do the rest.

# A Tour of the Village

In days gone by, men approached the 'Holy Land of Walsingham', as they called it, by various routes but for the most part, they would come through the little town of Fakenham. Nowadays, we may by-pass the little town, but whether we come from King's Lynn or Norwich, we will make for it, and then follow the road marked 'Walsingham; Wells-next-the-Sea', a turn off the Lynn road. Some three miles along this road is the village of East Barsham, and the magnificent Tudor manor house lies below us as we come into the village. Built in the reign of Henry VII, it is a fine example of highly decorated Tudor brickwork. It is not very large, and has no great estate attached to it. In spite of its romantic appearance, it has had no regular occupant in recent years, and it is not usually possible to visit the interior, so we must admire it from the hill. All Saints' church is all that remains of a larger building, which many find attractive for its primitive simplicity. Some pieces of medieval glass are incorporated in its windows, and there is a notable monument to a member of the Calthorp family, well known in the district in the seventeenth century, dating from 1640. (It was at East Barsham manor that Henry VIII is reported to have stayed on his pilgrimage to Walsingham.) The road to the left, past the church, leads to the tiny village of West Barsham, which has a small but beautifully restored — almost completely rebuilt — church of the Assumption. Some eleventh century work remains in the nave. The church may be difficult to find as it is hidden behind the big house. Turn right at the bottom of the hill from East Barsham, and the road leads to North Barsham, another tiny village beside the river Stiffkey, whose church has a seventeenth century pulpit and a thirteenth century font. The road alongside the stream leads to the Chapel of St. Catherine, or Slipper Chapel.

However, the visitor is more likely to continue on the road through East Barsham towards Walsingham. Houghton-in-the Dale, or Houghton St. Giles, the next village, has a small fifteenth century church with an attractive screen. This is the beginning of the parish of Walsingham. Very soon, on the left hand side of the road, there is a signpost reading 'Unbridged Ford' (a common notice in Norfolk). One may cross the Stiffkey by this ford, or by the adjacent bridge, and go thence to the Slipper Chapel, which is a short distance to the left. It may be wiser to continue along the road almost to the entrance to the village of Walsingham and retrace one's steps, as the signpost directs, to the 'Slipper Chapel & Shrine'.

**The 'Slipper Chapel'**

The small chapel was built in the late fourteenth or early fifteenth century, and, quite apart from its associations, is one of the loveliest medieval buildings in Walsingham. Dedicated to St Catherine of Alexandria, it is widely believed that pilgrims would remove their shoes here and walk the last mile to the shrine barefoot. Modern pilgrims, especially the younger, have frequently been known to follow their example. It is reported of Henry VIII, the evil genius of Walsingham, that he walked barefoot from Barsham manor, about a mile further! Niches on the west front of the chapel hold statues of the Blessed Virgin and the Archangel Gabriel. Inside, the statue of Our Lady of Walsingham is venerated, and like all such statues is derived from the figure depicted on the medieval seal of the Priory in the British Museum. It was crowned in 1954 with an exceedingly precious crown; but this is seldom seen. The window over the altar commemorates the definition of the doctrine of the Assumption by Pope Pius XII in 1950, and was the last work of Geoffrey Webb, a noted stained glass artist of his day. A cloister leads to the small Holy Ghost chapel. Returning outside, the fourteen large wooden crosses were those carried in the pilgrimage for peace in 1947, completed by a fifteenth, commemorating the resurrection, carried from Milton Keynes and added in 1982. This stands near the roadside door of the Chapel of Reconciliation, the largest building on the site, consecrated by the Bishop of East Anglia in 1982. In the past, the design of the modern buildings on the site has frequently been criticised, but this chapel fits admirably into the countryside. It is designed after the pattern of a Norfolk barn, and local materials and craftsmanship were extensively used in its construction. The glass was made at Langham, a nearby village. The altar, of polished Aberdeen granite, was originally consecrated in 1973, and the walls of the chapel can be removed so that it acts as an open air altar when numbers require it.

A service area behind the Slipper Chapel, provides for the needs of pilgrims, and a priest's house, designed to match the architecture and materials of the chapel, dates from the restoration in 1897. There is adequate parking space for coaches and cars. The whole site is continually being developed and improved.

From the Slipper Chapel, follow the river Stiffkey (it is a very pleasant walk) along the 'holy mile' into Walsingham, and you may well meet a procession going in the opposite direction.

# The village street and parish church

The village is made attractive by the number of old houses, dating from the earlier centuries, which survive. Many are built of brick and flint, the typical Norfolk materials, with old tiled roofs and oak beams. Also prominent are the rounded Dutch gables often found in East Anglia. On the left, at the entrance to the village, are the remains of the Franciscan Friary, dating from the fifteenth century. Parts of the guest house, gateway, kitchen walls and cloisters may be seen. It is open at certain specified times (notice on the gate), which should be respected as it is a private residence. To the right, Church Street leads to the parish church of St Mary and All Saints. It dates mostly from the fourteenth and fifteenth centuries and visitors are frequently surprised by the interior, which is white and new. In 1961 a disastrous fire completely gutted the interior, and the present restoration was carried out under the direction of Laurence King. It is possible to appreciate its light, colour and beauty, but yet to regret the disappearance of the homely sense of an old parish church. The Seven Sacrament font survived the fire, and is one of the finest in the country. Part of a seventeenth century tomb also survived, and was moved from the Guilds' Chapel (north side) to its present position after the fire. The chancel was shortened by a screen to provide vestry accommodation and the colourful high altar provides a background to the recently installed nave altar, which provides for contemporary liturgical requirements. The figures of the great rood at the head of the nave were designed by Sir Ninian Comper, and originally hung in the chapel of the Sisters of Bethany in Lloyd Square, London. The colourful and impressive east window is by John Hayward. It depicts the annunciation of the Archangel Gabriel to the Blessed

Virgin in the lower lights, the Shrine at Walsingham and the Blessed Virgin with the old church on fire at her feet, and the restored church in her arms. Above are saints associated with Walsingham: St Augustine, St Francis, St James (the patron of pilgrims) and St Thomas Becket, whose shrine at Canterbury was the other great English centre of pilgrimage. Notable royal pilgrims figure on the other side, including the sinister figure of Henry VIII. The window is a memorial to Fr Hope Patten, who is commemorated also in a small chapel of St Hugh above the south porch, itself restored in 1969. The south chapel is dedicated to St Catherine. On a pillar in the north (Guilds') chapel, a small statue of Our Lady of Walsingham marks the spot where the statue, at present in the Anglican shrine, was venerated until the present Holy House was built. It was moved there on 15 October 1931. The reredos in this chapel is by G.F. Bodley, a notable church architect of the late nineteenth century, and was presented to the church and moved here in 1979. Fr Patten, the restorer of the (Anglican) Shrine, who did so much to revive devotion to an interest in Walsingham, is buried outside the main door of the church.

Descending once more to street level, it is possible by turning to the right to walk along a 'Sunken Road' to the Shrine. This is a pleasant walk with meadows on one side, and the grounds of 'Walsingham Abbey', the large house built originally from materials from the Priory, on the other. Later there are woods, which, in early spring, are white with snowdrops. For a short visit, however, it is better to return to the main street of the village.

## Friday market

A few yards from Church Street, a turn to the left leads into Friday Market. On the left of this road stands the Methodist Church. The Methodist Society in Walsingham was founded in 1779, and the present building dates from 1793/4. It is the oldest Methodist church still in use in East Anglia, a square, brick building, with arched windows and pillared portico. The interior is in the plain simple style of eighteenth century Methodist preaching houses. The gallery has its original pews, although the arrangements downstairs date from Victorian days.

For the most part, however, the Friday market is the centre of administration and accommodation for Roman Catholic pilgrims. Elmham House is a hostel and social centre, to which special accommodation for the sick has been added. The Pilgrim Bureau is housed in the old Grammar School. The small R.C. Church of the Annunciation also stands in the Friday Market and has a replica of the statue placed in the church in King's Lynn in 1897. The Black Lion Hotel is the largest of the surviving inns of old Walsingham, and has a great deal of fifteenth century stonework.

The road beside the Black Lion, Market Lane, leads to the former railway station, and the station yard, at times used as a coach park. The station building has been artistically converted into the Russian Orthodox Church of St Seraphim, and was blessed by the Russian Archbishop Nikodem in 1967. It is under the care of the Skete (or Monastery) of St Seraphim whose house is now in a nearby village. The liturgy is celebrated every Sunday, but the building is too small and the former Methodist church in Great Walsingham, dating from 1892, has been acquired by the Orthodox community. At St Seraphim's, icons of Our Lady of Walsingham are painted and sold, a change from the more familiar images and pictures. The church is usually open.

## Old houses

It is well worth while to return to the High Street, for several old houses may be seen. One, on the left (no.17), Dow House, dating from the sixteenth century, is probably one of the medieval guest houses. On the right hand side of the street, are several attractive buildings. One (no.20) has a simple Georgian facade which hides an almost complete medieval house, and a little further (no.24), an excellent example of the Dutch gable (originally there were two gables, one, unfortunately, having been removed). The Oxford Stores public house is a sixteenth century building with interesting work in the brick and flint and carved brackets. On the opposite side of the street, beyond the Priory Gate, is a row of four interesting old houses, built, in order, in the fifteenth (no.48), eighteenth (no.50), seventeenth (no.52), and sixteenth (no.54) centuries.

## Priory ruins

To return, however, to the Priory Gate. It is the original gatehouse to the Augustinian Priory destroyed at the Reformation, and dates from the fifteenth century. Although the niches are empty, one figure, in the top centre, remains — the head of a man, said by some to represent one of the monks guarding the Priory. The grounds are in private hands, but admission is allowed on certain days on payment of a small fee. Straight ahead, is the great east window of the priory church, which is the most impressive remain on the site, and one can make out the lines of the priory church. The building was completed by 1390. It had a nave of six bays, and a central tower. There may have been a west tower, but it was probably never completed. The great east window, of course, stood at the end of the choir. Excavation seems to have settled the vexed question of the actual location of the medieval Holy House containing the greatly venerated statue. It was, apparently, on the north side of the priory church, and approached through a passage. During the fifteenth century, 'new work' was undertaken to protect the Holy House, and details of the structure were recorded by William of Worcester (1479); the Holy House, he tells us, was 23ft.6in. x 12ft.10in., measurements which were followed when the modern Anglican shrine was built. Erasmus, the Flemish humanist, visited Walsingham at the beginning of the sixteenth century, and left a description of the shrine. There was no light, save that of tapers, and it gleamed with the reflection of jewels, gold and silver, 'You would say it was the mansion of the saints'. The statue stood on the gospel (north) side of the altar in the chapel.

Close to the modern house, are the ruins of the monastic buildings. The monks' refectory is discernible, and a short flight of steps leads to the rostrum, or pulpit, for reading during meals.

In recent years, the priory grounds have once again become the scene of great religious events. The big pilgrimages, Anglican, Roman Catholic, and ecumenical, culminate in services on the site of the old priory church, with an altar set up on the site of the Augustinians' high altar.

Behind the great east window, and under a small arch, are the twin wells and bath, believed to be those associated with the medieval shrine. In later days they were spoken of as 'Wishing Wells', but modern visitors and pilgrims will probably prefer to make their devotions at the well in the Anglican Shrine.

## The 'Common Place'

Returning out of the Priory Gate into the High Street, it is a short distance to the Common Place, one of the quaintest and most interesting squares in Norfolk, surrounded by ancient buildings. The Bull Inn, at the bottom end of the place, is a fifteenth century building behind a nineteenth century facade, and keeps much of the atmosphere of the old country inn, so is very popular with pilgrims seeking refreshment. At the opposite end of the square the sixteenth century building with an archway, was formerly the Swan Inn. The Office of the Anglican Shrine is housed in one of the old houses on the south side, and on the north, is the old Shirehall (fifteenth century) now housing a small museum.* In the centre of the square stands the medieval pump (early sixteenth century), probably originally surmounted by a cross but now by a fire basket in which a beacon is still lighted on great occasions of national rejoicing.

## The Anglican Shrine

Following the road beside the Bull Inn will lead to the Anglican Shrine. The buildings on the left are part of the hospice for pilgrims, first the newer buildings, then the adapted and modernised cottages. A large gateway leads into the gardens of the Shrine, but it is better to go further down to the front entrance. (There is a special

---

* It has the furnishings of a George III country courthouse, including a prisoners' lock-up.

gate for the disabled, which can be opened on request.) A cobbled courtyard in front of the building reproduces that recorded of the medieval shrine. The facade and campanile have been criticised as being Italianate and unsuitable for a Norfolk village, but the remainder of the building is very local, and with the passage of time even the facade has mellowed. When the whole is floodlit, it makes an attractive sight. In the porch, on the left, is a small statue of Richeldis de Faverches who, according to the Walsingham story, saw the apparition which caused the shrine to be built. The atmosphere of the interior is sometimes found to be confusing, but it is well to remember that it was deliberately planned to recreate the atmosphere of a medieval church as the planners imagined it to have been. It is explicitly recorded by Erasmus that there was no daylight inside the holy house, and there is none in the new house which Hope Patten created in the 1930's. Light came originally from the central lantern. The fact that the church seems overcrowded will also be understood by those familiar with the furnishing of churches in past ages. The present authorities of the Shrine introduced more light into the building but have decided, wisely one imagines, to leave the main church alone, and to give expression to the more severe taste of a later generation elsewhere.

Inside the church one is faced by the altar of the Annunciation, and by turning left can follow the sequence of the remaining fourteen. (Charts are usually available. Remember that each altar has a patron saint or saints, and commemorates an event in the life of Christ or his Mother.)

The well, whose water is used for the blessing of pilgrims, was discovered when the Shrine was built. The reliquary holds the relics of St Vincent, and the effigy beside the well is of Fr Hope Patten, in whose memory this cloister was built. The Holy House is on the right and the innumerable lamps and candles carry the names of those places, causes and people who ask for prayers. Entering the Holy House, the statue is above the altar, whose frontal, reredos and canopy were designed by Sir Ninian Comper.

To follow the sequence of the altars etc., it is better to go out by the door through which one entered, and continue along the north side. The stalls are those of the Guardians of the Shrine, and the names of their occupants, past and present, are inscribed on them. Go behind the high altar. Upstairs is the chapel where the Blessed Sacrament is reserved, and visitors are asked not to go there except for prayer. It may be seen from the nave of the church. On the south side, another staircase leads to the Orthodox Chapel, which was blessed in 1938. It is a pan-Orthodox chapel, under the care of the skete (or monastery) of St Seraphim, and in the jurisdiction of the Russian Patriarchate. There has been an Orthodox presence in Walsingham ever since the statue was moved to the Shrine in 1931. The cloister on the south side (dating from 1972) allows light into the building, and it is possible to go out by the doors of the cloister and to see the foundations of some medieval building, of uncertain purpose, which have been left exposed.

## The shrine grounds

The Stations of the Cross start in this small garden (nos. 1 & 2); then it is necessary to go through the south end of the Shrine, nos. 3 & 4 are at the back of the church. The remainder are in the gardens, nos. 10-13 being on the little hill marked with three large crosses. The 14th is a reproduction of the Sepulchre, and the 15th station (of the resurrection) is nearby.

The octagonal building in the Shrine grounds is the chapel of St Michael and All Souls, which belongs to the Guild of All Souls and, although attached to the Shrine, is a separate foundation. Here the departed are remembered every day. The chapel was designed by Laurence King, who was also responsible for the restoration of the parish church after the fire of 1961. The large outdoor altar was the gift of Lord Halifax, a well known layman who died in 1935. It was brought here from Goldthorpe in Yorkshire, and is used when numbers are too great for the shrine church. The pilgrim hospice is on the left hand side of the gardens, and their refectory is at the top. On the right, on the same level as the Shrine church, is a converted barn which is now a hall for the use of pilgrims or for meetings. Beyond this, but marked 'Private' is the College of St Augustine where the shrine clergy live. A view of part of it may be had from Knight Street, but the date stone (1727) is not part of the original structure which is probably some two hundred years older. Beyond the pilgrim refectory at the top of the gardens is the new (1985) St Joseph's wing for the sick and disabled, and beyond this again, the Priory of Our Lady where the Sisters of the Community of St Margaret who work for the Shrine have their home. This, of course, is also strictly private.

During the summer there is usually someone on duty

in the shrine church who will answer questions and arrange for any ministrations visitors may want. To return outside the church, we are at the beginning of Knight Street. This has kept alive the memory of one of the more famous stories attached to the medieval shrine. It was reported that a certain knight, fleeing from his pursuers, tried to seek sanctuary under the protection of the church and invoking our Lady of Walsingham found himself safe within the Priory. The original gate has long since disappeared, and the present replacement dates from the early nineteenth century, but the street and a small cafe called the 'Knight's Gate' still exist.

**Great Walsingham**

By continuing along Knight Street, past the war memorial, along the Wells road, one may reach Great Walsingham, by-passing the modern housing estate on the left and taking a road to the right alongside the village school. St Peter's church is on the left. It has lost its chancel, but is an attractive country church, dating from the fourteenth century. (Was it, one wonders, reduced in size after the Black Death — like so many other Norfolk churches or merely neglected at a later date?) It has all the atmosphere of a country church, and so contrasts with the almost suburban smartness of the restored St Mary's, Little Walsingham, and should certainly not be missed. The wood of the pews and the arch-braced roof have mellowed to a beautiful tone, and the church bells are reputed to be among the oldest in Britain — one may be *the* oldest. The path leads over a ford, with footbridge for pedestrians, into the village of Great Walsingham, outgrown since the early middle ages by its 'Little' sister. This has caused the very pleasant village green, and the quiet street remote from the throngs of pilgrims, to be neglected. By turning right in the village, one may return, again past some of the modern housing of Walsingham, to the Shrine.

# Further Afield

The car owner, or the hardened walker, while in the district, may seize the opportunity of seeing some of its other notable, but less frequently visited, monuments.

The road from the war memorial, at right angles to the Wells Road, leads to the Creakes (7m). North Creake church has a fifteenth century hammerbeam roof and an Easter sepulchre. South Creake's church of the Assumption has been more carefully restored, and has a hammerbeam roof with winged angels, and a fifteenth century rood screen and pulpit. It is particularly well kept, and the beauty of this (mainly) perpendicular building can be fully appreciated.

Little Snoring, on the road to Norwich, has one of the round, flint towers often found in Norfolk — in this case detached from the church. Great Snoring church has more of interest but the glory of the village is the Old Rectory (now a restaurant), a magnificent Tudor house dating from 1525. Great Ryburgh (reached by a one mile deviation from the Norwich road) has what may well be the oldest of the Norfolk flint towers, topped by a later, octagonal, belfry (fourteenth century?). The church is cruciform, and its restoration represents some of the earliest work of Sir Ninian Comper (1912).

It is worth while making an expedition into the heart of rural Norfolk, persevering through the village to the hamlet of Gateley. The church retains its medieval screen, complete with figures, only mildly vandalised in the sixteenth century. They include King Henry VI, Sir John Schorne, a thirteenth century cleric who cured ague and gout, and so is depicted conjuring the devil into a boot, and 'S Puella of Ridebowne', a lady otherwise unknown. So remote is Gateley, that it is not always possible to track down the key to the church, but in the same area, one may discover the remains of the Saxon cathedral at North Elmham, and a fine church, also with screen. At Langham is a Carmelite Convent, dedicated to Our Lady of Walsingham. The chapel may be visited. In King's Lynn, the Roman Catholic church of Our Lady of the Annunciation is in London Road, with the chapel of 1897 intact. The museum of King's Lynn has an interesting collection of pilgrim badges, some of which depict Our Lady of Walsingham.

Binham Priory, 'very nearly the most interesting monastic remains in Norfolk' (Shell Guide), has excellent Norman work, with early English arches. There is a seven sacrament font. It should not be missed.

# To be a Pilgrim

If you know all about pilgrimage you may skip this section, but there must be many who feel they would like to make the venture for the first time. It is probably best to go with an organized party — perhaps a church in your neighbourhood organizes pilgrimages to Walsingham. You would be very welcome to join one of their parties if you contact the organizer, and if you could get to know one or two others who are going before you start, it would make it easier. A pilgrimage is an act of faith, and a pilgrimage to Walsingham a demonstration of our belief that God the Son was born of Mary as a little child. We do not hold our Christian faith in isolation, we share it with our fellow Christians — that is why we are brought into a brotherhood or 'church', and on the journey to any shrine we help and encourage one another. It is quite likely that there will be people very different from ourselves in the party, and people from very different parts of the country when we get to Walsingham. All the better: we so easily come to think that 'Christian' means like us! A number of people from overseas *do* come to Walsingham, but it is primarily visited by British people. Other pilgrimage centres are much more international, and mixing with men and women from different lands makes us realize a little more what we mean when we say in the Creed that the Church is 'Catholic', but even the different accents and different backgrounds of the people we meet here will help.

In spite of this, there may be some who want to make a private pilgrimage. Have no hesitation about it — you will be very welcome. Write in good time to the office of one or other of the shrines, (addresses on p. 51) or to a hotel in the village and book a room. Do not ask for accommodation at weekends in the summer, for it is always in great demand, and probably every bed in the village, and sometimes for miles round, has been booked months before. Anglicans naturally tend to stay at the Anglican hospice, and Roman Catholics in the R.C. accommodation, but they help one another and are not exclusive. If you are disabled, or are taking with you someone who needs special care, say so when you write, for both authorities provide for such people and are very glad to welcome them.

Those who have only seen Walsingham on a special occasion, when it is crowded with people, find it hard to think of it as a place of prayer and need to come back. Those who come by themselves, miss the sense of togetherness and the inspiration which a big pilgrimage gives. Both quiet and crowds are important.

You will be able to join in many of the activities of a pilgrimage party which may be there at the same time as yourself e.g. the processions and Stations of the Cross, and there are many opportunities of taking part in the Eucharist and receiving Holy Communion. Apart from that, allow yourself plenty of time for private prayer and intercession, and make sure penitence has a part in your prayers. There may be a service of penance while you are there, and there are many opportunities of receiving the sacrament of reconciliation. You may need the sacrament of the sick and/or a special blessing. Anglicans will be sprinkled with the water at the Shrine. In any case, make a visit to the 'other' shrine, which ever it may be, and pray for the visible unity of Christ's people. You are following in the footsteps of cardinals, archbishops and bishops when you do, and your prayers for this great end are very important. Try not to make your visit too rushed, and allow time to see something of this remarkable place and what goes on there.

# Getting to Walsingham

### By road

Walsingham is approached by road from the west (King's Lynn), the south or the east (Norwich) and is five miles from Fakenham.

*From King's Lynn* follow A418 to Fakenham, just before the A148 enters Fakenham take the B1105 which is clearly signposted 'Walsingham'.

*From Norwich* follow the A1067 towards Fakenham, pass through Fakenham following the signs for King's Lynn. Immediately on leaving the built up area of Fakenham take the B1105 which is clearly marked 'Walsingham'.

*From London and the South* follow the M11 towards Newmarket, then the A11 and Stump Cross. At Barton Mills roundabout take the A1065 through Brandon and Swaffham to Fakenham. By-pass Fakenham to the King's Lynn–Fakenham road (A148). Turn right on the A148 for about 100 yards then left on the B1105 which is signposted 'Walsingham'.

### By rail

The nearest stations are Norwich and King's Lynn both 27 miles away.

### By bus

There are regular buses between Norwich and Fakenham, also King's Lynn and Fakenham. Local bus companies operate services between Fakenham and Walsingham. For further details, please contact the Bureau or Shrine Office.

**Coach**

There is a daily National Coach service from London to Fakenham (5 miles from Walsingham), for further details contact the Pilgrim Bureau, Shrine Office or National Express Coaches.

**Taxi**

A 'Pilgrim Taxi Service' is on call 24 hours, distance no object. Telephone: Walsingham (032872 483).

ADDRESSES for reserving accommodation and other enquiries:

| | |
|---|---|
| Roman Catholic pilgrimages: | The Pilgrim Bureau, Friday Market, Walsingham, Norfolk NR22 6EE. (Tel: Walsingham 217) |
| Anglican pilgrimages: | The Bursar, The Shrine Office, Walsingham, Norfolk NR22 6EE. (Tel: Walsingham 255) |

## Pilgrimage time tables

Most people, however, probably come with an organized pilgrimage. Arrangements at the Anglican and Roman Catholic shrines are as follows:
Weekend pilgrimage at the Anglican Shrine:

> Sung Mass at 6 p.m. on Saturday
> Candlelight procession in honour of
>   Our Lady 8.15 p.m.
> Sprinkling at the well 3 p.m. on Sunday
> Final procession 4.30 p.m.

A first visit to the Holy House, Stations of the Cross, intercessions, and a final visit are arranged by individual parties. (Mass daily at 7.30 a.m., and at other times as arranged.) Shrine Prayers are said every day at 6 p.m. (Saturdays 5.00 p.m.). These include intercessions sent in from all over the country and the world, as well as those which pilgrims and visitors have requested. A box is provided in which petitions may be placed. Day pilgrimages are organized to allow time for most of the devotions, except the processions which take place only at weekends, but can be arranged at other times as necessary.

Roman Catholic weekend pilgrimages are usually planned to start on Friday evenings. They include a procession from the village to the Slipper Chapel to a

> Liturgy of Penitence and Reconciliation
> Mass is celebrated daily at the Chapel or in the
> Chapel of Reconciliation at midday (and also at 5 p.m.)
> One hour's adoration
> Intercessions and Rosary in the Slipper Chapel
> Stations of the Cross should be made privately.

At both shrines, the sacrament of the sick is given by arrangement.

## Special days and occasions

March 25, the feast of the Annunciation and August 15, the feast of the Assumption, are both important days in Walsingham for which special arrangements will be made. On August 14, there is a torchlight procession round all the churches of the village. (The Annunciation is sometimes transferred when it would fall in Holy Week or Easter.) At the Anglican Shrine : The National Pilgrimage is on the Spring Bank Holiday, i.e. the last Monday in May. This includes an open air Mass (usually in the grounds of Walsingham Abbey) and a great procession through the village.

Parliamentary Pilgrimage, when Christian members of both houses of parliament come together to pray for their work. This is completely ecumenical, and special arrangements are made at both shrines. It is usually held in May.

'Student Cross', again an ecumenical pilgrimage, takes place at Easter. Students from universities and colleges anywhere in the country are welcome, and the Shrine authorities can put them in touch with the organizers.

Pilgrimage for the disabled.

At the Roman Catholic Shrine the National Pilgrimage is at the beginning of September.

The pilgrimage of the Union of Catholic Mothers on the first Tuesday in July.

Pilgrimage for the Sick in early July.

# SOME PRAYERS AND DEVOTIONS

## The 'Mysteries' of the Rosary

*The Joyful Mysteries*
1. The Annunciation
2. The Visitation
3. The Birth of Jesus
4. The Presentation in the Temple
5. The Finding in the Temple

*The Sorrowful Mysteries*
1. The Agony in the Garden
2. The Scourging
3. The Crowning with Thorns
4. The Carrying of the Cross
5. The Death on the Cross

*The Glorious Mysteries*
1. The Resurrection
2. The Ascension
3. The Coming of the Holy Spirit
4. The Assumption of Our Lady
5. The Coronation of Our Lady

**The Stations, or Way, of the Cross**

1. Jesus is condemned to death
2. Jesus receives his cross
3. Jesus falls the first time
4. Jesus meets his mother
5. Simon of Cyrene helps to carry the cross
6. St Veronica wipes the face of Jesus
7. Jesus falls the second time
8. Jesus speaks to the women of Jerusalem
9. Jesus falls the third time
10. Jesus is stripped of his garments
11. Jesus is nailed to the cross
12. Jesus dies on the cross
13. Jesus is taken down from the cross
14. Jesus' body is laid in the tomb
(15. Jesus rises from the dead).

You may make the way of the cross by yourself, and stop at each 'station' to say suitable prayers.

**The Angelic Salutation, or Hail Mary**

Hail Mary, full of grace, the Lord is with thee.
Blessed art thou among women and blessed is the fruit of thy womb Jesus. Holy Mary, Mother of God, pray for us sinners, now, and at the hour of our death. *Amen*.

## The Angelus

V. The angel of the Lord declared to Mary
R. And she conceived by the Holy Spirit   Luke 1.28
                Hail Mary . . .

V. Behold the handmaid of the Lord
R. Be it done to me according to your word   Luke 1.38
                Hail Mary . . .

V. The Word was made flesh
R. And dwelt among us   John 1.14
                Hail Mary . . .

We beseech thee, O Lord, pour thy grace into our hearts, that as we have known the incarnation of thy Son, Jesus Christ, by the message of an angel, so by his cross and passion we may be brought to the glory of his resurrection. Through Christ our Lord.

*Amen.*

Pour forth, we beseech you, O Lord, your grace into our hearts, that we, to whom the incarnation of Christ your Son was made known by the message of an angel, may by his passion and cross be brought to the glory of his resurrection, through the same Christ our Lord.

*Amen.*

**Magnificat** Luke 1: 46-55

My soul glorifies the Lord: my spirit rejoices in God my Saviour.
He looks on his servant in her lowliness: henceforth all ages will call me blessed.

The Almighty works marvels for me: Holy is his name!
His mercy is from age to age: on those who fear him.

He puts forth his arm in strength: and scatters the proud-hearted
He casts the mighty from their thrones: and raises the lowly.

He fills the starving with good things: sends the rich away empty.

He protects Israel, his servant, remembering his mercy
The mercy promised to our fathers: to Abraham and his sons for ever.

## An ancient prayer, usually attributed to Erasmus

O Alone of all women. Mother and Virgin, Mother most happy, Virgin most pure, now we, sinful as we are, come to see thee who art all pure, we salute thee, we honour thee as how we may with our humble offerings; may thy Son grant us, that imitating thy most holy manners, we also, by the grace of the Holy Ghost may deserve spiritually to conceive the Lord Jesus in our inmost soul, and once conceived never to lose him.

## Prayer to Our Lady of Walsingham

O Mary, recall the solemn moment when Jesus, your divine Son, dying on the cross, confided us to your maternal care. You are our Mother, we desire ever to remain your devout children.

Let us therefore feel the effects of your powerful intercession with Jesus Christ. Make your name again glorious in this place once renowned throughout our land by your visits, favours, and many miracles.

Pray, O holy Mother of God, for the conversion of England, restoration of the sick, consolation for the afflicted, repentance for sinners, peace to the departed. O blessed Mary, Mother of God, Our Lady Walsingham, intercede for us. *Amen.*

## The oldest known prayer to the Blessed Virgin (probably dating from the 4th century)

We fly to your patronage, O holy Mother of God. Despise not our petitions in our necessities, but deliver us from all dangers, O glorious and blessed Virgin.

**Prayer for Unity**

Lord Jesus Christ, you said to your apostles peace I leave with you, my peace I give to you. Look not on our sins but the faith of your church, and grant her the peace and unity of your kingdom, where you live and reign for ever and ever.  *Amen.*

**Orthodox prayers to the Mother of God**

O unfailing Intercessor of Christians, O constant Mediatress before the Creator, despise not the cry of us sinners, but of thy goodness, come speedily to the help of us who in faith call upon thee. Hasten to offer swift intercession and prayer for us, O Mother of God, who ever intercedest for those who honour thee.

More honourable than the Cherubim and incomparably more glorious than the Seraphim, thou who in virginity didst bear God the Word, thee, true Mother of God, we magnify.